City of Edinburgh

To the first-time visitor Edinburgh is, indeed, an experience unlike any other. The Castle, visible as it is from almost every point, stands guard over a city that would not have existed without its mighty presence. In its shadow and stretching away down the hill is the Old Town whose grey tenements, wynds, courts and closes speak its secrets, its mysteries, its stories of courage, roguery and passion. From the Castle, down the Royal Mile to the Palace of Holyroodhouse, serene in the shelter of Arthur's Seat, Scotland's turbulent history is clearly evident all around.

To the north, across Princes Street, a quieter mood prevails in the Georgian grace of the New Town, with its echoes of the Age of Reason. Yet this harmony, like all else in Edinburgh, owes its allegiance to its first founder on the hill, still intact and impregnable.

The Castle on a loftie Rocke is so strongly grounded, bounded, and founded, that by force of man it can never be confounded; the Foundation and Walls are unpenetrable, the Rampiers impregnable, the Bulwarkes invincible, no way but one to it is or can be possible to be made passable.

JOHN TAYLOR, 1618

ABOVE: *The dramatic and imposing castle site has probably been fortified since the Iron Age, though the present buildings date from the reign of Malcolm Canmore (1085–93).*

RIGHT: *Edinburgh Castle esplanade, leading to the gatehouse entrance which is flanked by statues of Robert the Bruce and William Wallace.*

Impregnable it may have been, but most of the Castle that we see today is not as old as the 11th-century Chapel of St. Margaret, built by the pious Queen Margaret, wife of Malcolm III. The Chapel alone remained when the rest of the Castle was razed to the ground by Thomas Ranulph, Earl of Moray, in 1313. Over the centuries it has served as a 'Gunners Storehouse' and a 'shop for the sale of trashy articles to trippers'. It was finally re-dedicated in 1934, having been restored and refurbished.

The rest of the Castle of Edinburgh, which has been at the centre of Scottish life for nine centuries (and is now the most visited of Scottish Monuments), has an

RIGHT: *A tribute to the Scots Greys above Princes Street Gardens, with the Castle in the background.*

equally chequered history. It was the Scottish equivalent of the Tower of London; its position made it a natural prison. Many illustrious men endured imprisonment, torture and death there, in pursuit of passionate or violent causes. For example, James III's brother, Alexander, Duke of Albany, was imprisoned in David's Tower in 1479. He and his servant escaped by killing the Captain of the Guard and three soldiers when they were drunk, and lowering themselves down the walls on a rope of sheets. The Marquis of Argyll was beheaded by the Maiden (the Scottish guillotine) in 1661, for having been a Parliamentarian sympathizer. The political climate changed and an English gentleman, Henry Neville Payne, was tortured by boot and thumb screws for having Jacobite sympathies in the 1690s. The Earl of Crawford reported that 'it was surprising that flesh and blood could, without fainting, endure the heavy penance he was in for two hours'.

Prisoners of the Napoleonic and other French wars were interred in the vaults beneath the Great Hall where their names are still carved in stone. One of them was a hero in Robert Louis Stevenson's novel, *St. Ives*. Their lot was less severe than that of earlier prisoners – the citizens of Edinburgh helped them by contributing towards a fund set up for their relief, and bought the small toys, snuff and trinket boxes, that the prisoners made. They must have been well-treated because when released they wrote to the Governor thanking him for their good treatment.

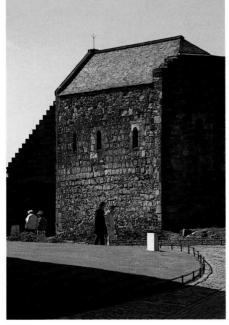

FAR LEFT: *One of the window frames in St. Margaret's Chapel, now filled with modern stained glass.*

LEFT: *St. Margaret's Chapel stands on the highest part of the Castle Rock; it is the oldest building in the Castle and in Edinburgh. Queen Margaret, its founder from whom the chapel took its name, was canonized in the 13th century.*

RIGHT: *The one o'clock gun is fired every day from Mill's Mount Battery artillery platform.*

BELOW: *Mons Meg dates from the 15th century and was probably forged at Mons in Belgium; its construction is similar to that of 'Mad Marjory', the great cannon at Ghent. It is now on display in the vaults.*

The sieges of Edinburgh Castle are legion and legendary; their story is that of the turbulent history of Scotland. The first recorded use of artillery in the British Isles was in 1327 in the war of Edward II against the Scots, although siege cannons did not become part of the Scottish arsenal for some years.

The giant bombard, *Mons Meg*, has been surrounded by legend and romantic tales. It was, in fact, commissioned by Duke Philip of Burgundy in 1449. He, as uncle of the wife of King James II of Scotland, and having had no cause to use *Mons* in her first 8 years of life, gave the bombard to his niece's husband. To James, who was fascinated by cannon, it must have been an ideal gift. The arrival of *Mons* would have had a similar effect to that of a nuclear weapon in Europe in modern times – she was a huge, powerful and innovative weapon. Unfortunately,

James's fascination with cannon led to his death in 1460 as a result of standing too near one as it was discharged.

There are records of *Mons Meg* having been made ready for action in 1489 (under James III) and 1497 under James IV, but not of her having been fired. 'The first shot was fired as a salute on the day King James V was born' (*c.*1512). By 1513 giant bombards like *Mons* had become outdated and *Mons* after this time was used principally in the firing of salutes.

LEFT: *Looking past the Ross Fountain in Princes Street Gardens to the Castle. Before the New Town was developed, there was a considerable stretch of water, the Nor' Loch, where the Gardens now are.*

BELOW LEFT: *The 'Honours of Scotland' – the royal crown, sceptre and sword. The crown was refashioned for James V in the 16th century. The sceptre is the* oldest and was a gift from the Pope to James IV in 1494. The sword was presented by another pope in 1707.

BELOW: *The collection of arms and armour in the Great Hall. The most interesting feature is the great hammer-beam roof with human and animal masks at the ends of the beams and carved stone corbels supporting them.*

In a small room in the Palace, or King's Lodging, which James IV built on the Castle Rock, was born James VI of Scotland who became James I of England in 1603. The Scottish Crown, Sceptre and Sword of State are still kept in the King's Lodging, as they have been for many years. The Scottish United Services Museum, which contains a valuable collection of military relics, uniforms, medals, colours, trophies, decorations and weapons, is housed in part of the Palace.

The Great Hall was restored by James IV and was used as a Parliament Hall and a venue for State Banquets. Charles I dined there and, fifteen years later, Oliver Cromwell was entertained. Then for two centuries the Hall became a barracks and military hospital and was not restored to its former glory until William Nelson, the publisher, paid for its restoration in 1887.

LEFT: *St. Giles' Cathedral: the High Kirk of Edinburgh. Generally regarded as the mother church of Presbyterianism, it was consecrated by the Bishop of St. Andrews in 1243, although the four massive central pillars dating from around 1120 are the oldest parts of the present building. After the Reformation John Knox became its first minister. Charles II elevated it to the status of a cathedral.*

BELOW: *The roof of the Thistle Chapel, opened in 1911. The Knights of the Thistle, Scotland's chief order of chivalry, had their own chapel built in St. Giles' Cathedral.*

If Edinburgh Castle has been at the centre of Scottish life for nine centuries, St. Giles' Cathedral, the High Kirk of Edinburgh, has been the religious heart of Scotland for even longer.

In 854 there was a church on the site; it belonged to Lindisfarne, where Columba's monks first brought the Gospel from Iona. In 1150, the monks of St. Giles' were farming lands round about and a bigger church was built by the end of the century. That this first parish church of Edinburgh was dedicated to St. Giles, a saint popular in France, was probably due to the Auld Alliance of Scotland and France against the common enemy of England.

The widowed Queen of James II (he who was killed by one of his beloved cannon) in 1460 added considerably to St. Giles'; the chancel was added, the roof was heightened and the clerestory windows put in. The church grew in importance too and in 1467 a Papal Bull confirmed James III's proposal that it should become a Collegiate Church.

Merchant Guilds supported St. Giles'; some guild money, ship-dues and fines all went 'to the kirk werk'. Some guilds had their own chapels. Monarchs and nobles supported and enriched the church for varying reasons.

Scotland was a Catholic nation until the Reformation in the mid-16th century and the parish church of Edinburgh was central to the city's and the nation's religious turmoil.

It is doubtful whether anyone brought St. Giles' into greater prominence than John Knox, the fiery 'Trumpeter of God', who preached against Popery. 'He had the most part of the blame of all the troubles in Scotland since the murder of the Cardinal.'

This refers to a contemporary, Cardinal Beaton, who was murdered in 1546 by Scotsmen at his castle of St. Andrews, following the burning of the militant reformer, George Wishart, whom John Knox admired. After the Cardinal's murder Knox became a preacher – 'Others lopped the branches of the papistry, but he strikes at the root, to destroy the whole.'

When Wishart had been arrested he had, so Knox said, told him not to seek to join him in martyrdom, on the grounds that 'one is sufficient for a sacrifice'. This advice Knox never forgot, for he was (sensibly) convinced that he would do better service to his cause alive than dead, and he never allowed himself to be confronted with the terrible choice between the stake and recantation.

This follower of Calvin, the stern French philosopher who preached the doctrine of predestination in Geneva – that only the elect qualify for the Kingdom of God – spent time as a galley prisoner of the French and as a preacher in Geneva, Frankfurt and Newcastle, before being appointed Minister at St. Giles' in 1559. The publication of his tract 'The First Blast of the Trumpet against the Monstrous Regiment of Women' earned him the detestation of the Protestant Queen Elizabeth I. So incensed was she that she refused him passage through England when he returned to Scotland from Geneva. The Catholics, Mary Tudor and Mary of Guise (the mother of Mary Queen of Scots), were already targets at whom Knox levelled his verbal assaults.

FAR RIGHT: *A page of Knox's 'Blast' against female rulers, published at Geneva in 1558, with a singularly forthright paragraph.*

RIGHT: *The burning of George Wishart at St. Andrews, from a woodcut in Holinshed's Chronicles (1577). Wishart was a great inspiration to Knox.*

ABOVE: *Detail from a window in the John Knox House which depicts Knox with appropriate symbolism: the tower of St. Giles', grapes and grain (Holy Communion), emblems of Scotland and Edinburgh, an open Bible, a cross and serpent (St. John's Gospel, iii, 14) and the Lamb of God.*

LEFT, TOP and CENTRE: *The John Knox House as it was about 1760 and as it is today. It stands near the Netherbow gate which formerly separated Edinburgh from Canongate. It was occupied by one Knox long before the time of the reformer, whose association with it is not authenticated.*

THE FIRST BLAST
TO AWAKE WOMEN degenerate.

O promote a woman to beare rule, superioritie, dominion or empire aboue any realme, nation, or citie, is repugnāt to nature, côtumelie to God, a thing moſt contrarious to his reueled will and approued ordināce, and finallie it is the ſubuerſion of good order, of all equitie and iuſtice.

In the probation of this propoſition, I will not be ſo curious, as to gather what foeuer may amplifie, ſet furth, or decore the ſame, but I am purpoſed, euen as I haue ſpoken my conſcience in moſt plaine ād fewe wordes, ſo to ſtād content with a ſimple proofe of euerie membre, bringing in for my witneſſe Goddes ordinance in nature, his plaine will reueled in his worde, and the mindes of ſuch as be moſte ancient amongeſt godlie writers.

And firſt, where that I affirme the em-
B i

'The Congregation', as Knox's followers were called, interpreted his sermons as an incitement to iconoclasm and reacted accordingly. An attempted rebellion failed, Knox having to leave Edinburgh because it had become 'dangerous'. The cause of 'the Congregation' was saved from military catastrophe by English intervention and finally the treaty of Berwick in 1560 ensured protection for the Scots against the French.

Knox's aim was to create a reformed Church in Scotland, to banish 'popery', to strengthen democracy and to set up a system of comprehensive education. The religious transition was to take 130 years of struggle to achieve.

John Knox was to become a considerable thorn in the flesh of the Catholic Mary Stewart, who was Queen of Scotland before she was a week old, in 1542. She lived most of her first six years within the sturdy walls of Stirling Castle and the next ten in France. In 1558 she was married, in Notre Dame in Paris, to the French Dauphin Francis, a union welcomed by both France and Scotland who wished to keep England's ambitions in check. The English Queen, Mary Tudor, and the French King, Henry II, advanced the claim of his recently acquired daughter-in-law to be Queen of England. He contended that Mary Tudor's half-sister, Elizabeth, as the daughter of Anne Boleyn and Henry VIII, was illegitimate and therefore could not inherit the English throne.

When King Henry died in 1559, Mary Stewart reached the pinnacle of her career; queen-regnant of Scotland; queen-consort of France; queen-claimant of England.

But within a year she had abandoned her claim to the English throne and, as a childless widow, was of no account in France. Only Scotland was left to her and that had undergone the religious revolution of John Knox. Her good looks and stately bearing won Scottish hearts, her tragic young widowhood aroused their compassion, and her moderation, despite her own Catholicism, overcame their fears. For the first few years after her return to Scotland in 1561 Mary played the very difficult role of Catholic queen in a recently protestantised country with tact, charm and energy.

The marriage question was addressed again. Mary chose Henry Lord Darnley – a most suitable spouse it seemed. He had royal connections, good looks, charm, youth – and a pride and insensitivity which prevented him from being the support she needed. His jealousy of her advisers – first Moray and then Rizzio – led to a rebellion and then to a murder.

On the night of 9 March 1566, while Mary sat at supper in Holyroodhouse, Darnley unexpectedly entered the queen's apartments by means of the private stairway from his own suite on the floor below. Hardly had the queen's party, which included Rizzio, recovered from this unlooked for intrusion when the other conspirators followed by the same route, seized the secretary, dragged him struggling and protesting from the room and savagely stabbed him to death outside. The motives of the participants in this violent deed were varied. For Darnley it was a comparatively straightforward act of vengeance against the man who, he believed, had supplanted him in the queen's affections. For others of the murderers the victim was a low-born upstart who had risen too high in the kingdom and was ousting better men from the positions of influence to which their birth entitled them.

The murder of Rizzio solved nothing. With a party of nobles (which included Bothwell, whose staunch support at the time of Rizzio's murder had been invaluable to her) Mary, in late November, discussed the problem of her husband.

Darnley's death a year later is one of the most intractable mysteries of history, and every account of it leaves some loose ends. Even the way in which he died is not quite clear. The house, at Kirk o' Field in Edinburgh, in which he was resident on the night of 9–10 February 1567, was totally destroyed by an explosion at 2 a.m., but Darnley's body was found in a garden on the other side of the town wall, strangled!

What matters to Mary's story is not how Darnley died, nor who killed him, but what her contemporaries believed at the time. Popular report ascribed the leadership in the conspiracy against Darnley to James Hepburn, earl of Bothwell. When, therefore, a bare three months after the murder, on 15 May 1567, Mary married this same Bothwell, Scotland was scandalised. Before long, yet another conspiracy was formed, this time to 'free' the queen from Bothwell.

In contrast to the previous plots, this one had widespread support. The public reputation of the queen had been tarnished beyond recovery by her third marriage.

Mary was 'rescued' from Bothwell at Carberry Hill on 15 June 1567 and then very promptly shut up as a prisoner in lonely Lochleven Castle. There she was forced to sign a deed of abdication and to name a council of regency for her infant son.

On 2 May 1568 Mary escaped and made a desperate bid to regain her throne. She was defeated and never set foot in Scotland again. Elizabeth I was the reluctant author of her execution.

LEFT: *David Rizzio, Mary's Italian secretary. Rizzio was a talented poet and musician and used to play cards with Mary late into the night, thus earning the jealousy of her husband, Lord Darnley.*

BELOW: *The Queen's Bedchamber. Darnley's apartments were altered during Charles II's rebuilding of the Palace but the bed is an authentic period piece and was first inventoried in 1684.*

ABOVE: *The west front of the Palace of Holyroodhouse with the James IV Tower in the foreground (completed 1529–32). After the Restoration of 1660, Charles II decided to rebuild the Palace, though he never visited Scotland to see the result. Under the supervision of Sir William Bruce the modern Palace took shape from 1671–80: a southwest tower was built to complement the James IV Tower and an elegant façade erected between them.*

RIGHT: *Holyroodhouse as it appeared in 1647 during the reign of Charles I; from a drawing by Gordon of Rothiemay, in the Royal Collection.*

The story of Holyroodhouse, in which Mary Queen of Scots witnessed the horrific murder of her secretary by her husband, begins with the little chapel founded by Queen Margaret on the Castle rock. She had revered, in particular, the holy rood (or cross), kept in a golden casket and believed by her to be a part of Christ's cross. After her death her youngest son, David I (1084–1153), built the Augustinian Abbey of Holy Rood. (There are other legendary and more romantic foundation stories.) The monks cultivated the ground and brewed beer – to this day there are distilleries in the area – and so brought into being a community of farmers, craftsmen and traders around the Canon's Gate. (Canongate remained a separate burgh until the middle of the 19th century.)

The Abbey enjoyed many ecclesiastical triumphs and tragedies, culminating in the iconoclasm of the Reformation. Two hundred years later, an attempt to repair the roof with heavy stone flags resulted in a collapse during a hurricane, leaving Holyrood Abbey in 1768 the ruin we see today.

The Palace of Holyroodhouse, today the popular official Scottish residence of Britain's Royal Family, came into existence as a guest house for royal visitors, attached to the Abbey. James IV, in 1501, began to transform the guest house into a palace fit for his bride, Margaret Tudor, daughter of Henry VII, to live in. The extraordinary and turbulent events that have taken place there over the centuries include the notorious murder of David Rizzio, the harmless but hated favourite of Mary Queen of Scots.

A century later Holyrood saw one of the most splendid but grisly funerals in the history of Edinburgh. Oliver Cromwell had executed the royalist Marquis of Montrose for high treason; his limbs had been severed for display around the country. The Restoration of the Monarchy in 1660 reinstated the Marquis and, in 1661, he was retrieved – one of his legs was brought from Aberdeen, his head from a spike in Edinburgh, his other leg and his arms from Glasgow, Stirling and Perth, and the rest of his remains from the scaffold near the Tron Kirk. The bits and pieces lay in state

in the chapel of Holyrood for four months, and were then paraded through the streets in a coffin carried by 14 earls and buried in the High Kirk of St. Giles.

In 1544 an invading English army burned down most of the Palace and the Abbey. It was repaired, accidentally burnt down in 1650, rebuilt by Oliver Cromwell, and finally built as it now appears by Charles II in 1671. The palace that had begun life as a guesthouse associated with a medieval abbey had reached a classical climax in the 17th century on the orders of a king who never saw it.

In 1745 the Palace of Holyroodhouse was to play host to yet another splendid but blighted guest – the Young Pretender, Prince Charles Edward Stuart, who first had his father proclaimed James VIII, King of Scotland, England, France and Ireland, at the Mercat Cross, and then went on to occupy the Palace.

ABOVE, LEFT: *The ruined nave of Holyrood Abbey from the east.*

ABOVE: *The clock tower and main entrance to the Palace. The date 1680 indicates the completion of the building work carried out under Charles II.*

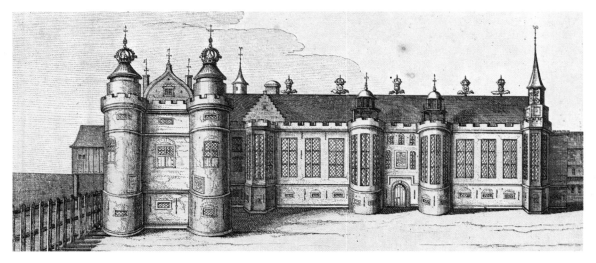

to present his case eloquently to others.

Charles set off with seven elderly but loyal companions for Scotland and reached Eriskay, in the Hebrides, on 23 July, 1745. Two days later he was on the mainland, entreating help from Donald Cameron of Lochiel, influential head of the Cameron Clan. Cameron counselled the Prince to 'be more temperate'. 'In a few days,' replied Charles, 'with the few friends that I have, I will erect the Royal Standard and proclaim to the people of Britain that Charles Stuart is come over to claim the crown of his ancestors, to win it, or perish in the attempt. Lochiel, who, as my father has often told me, was our firmest friend, may stay at home and learn from the newspapers the fate of his Prince.' Lochiel could not withstand this. 'No, I'll share the fate of my Prince,' he replied, 'and so shall every man over whom nature or fortune hath given me any power.'

Many more Highlanders joined the Camerons and the result was that Prince Charles was declared Regent and his father King of Scotland, and Charles appeared at the windows of the Palace of Holyroodhouse to acknowledge his people.

Consolidation of his position was needed; this was gained at the Battle of

ABOVE: *Prince Charles Edward Stuart. This portrait was painted in 1732 by Antonio David.*

RIGHT: *The battle of Culloden by David Morier. In this vivid impression of the battle, fought on Culloden Moor on 16 April 1746, the red-coated Hanoverian front-line absorbs the charge of the Camerons, Stewarts and Athollmen. Jacobite prisoners at Southwark were used as models for the Highland charge.*

James Stuart, the Old Pretender, Catholic brother of Charles II, always harboured dreams of being King of Scotland, even though his brother had been crowned king in Scotland as well as England and Scotland's role in royal affairs had become peripheral. James, however, found enough support in Scotland to launch three Jacobite rebellions there, in all of which he was defeated.

The birth of his son, Charles Edward Stuart, in 1720 was warmly acclaimed in Jacobite circles as a major achievement – surely great things would come of this.

By March 1744 Charles had the support of the French as he prepared to invade Scotland and reclaim her. Unfortunately, a fierce storm smashed the French fleet at Dunkirk and Charles had to make other plans. He would not spend a lifetime begging for French help – if necessary, he would start an uprising on his own. All he really had was an unshakable conviction in the justice of the Stuart cause and an ability

Prestonpans on 21 September. The ferocious Highland charge shattered the enemy's army in 8 minutes; Charles was magnanimous in victory – 'spare them, they are my father's subjects'.

London was the next target – the Highlanders met with no resistance but little enthusiasm from the English. A retreat was advised. A victorious battle at Falkirk followed which, in turn, led to the terrible skirmish with 'Butcher' Cumberland at Culloden Moor. The Jacobites were defeated and Bonnie Prince Charlie faced a five-months' wandering in the Western Highlands and Islands. There he met Flora Macdonald who was persuaded to help him escape 'over the sea to Skye', dressed as an Irish servant girl. He was still not safe – attempts to find him had intensified and on 20 September 1746 he left Scotland forever. He spent the rest of his life in exile, a pathetic figure. He is buried in Frascati, Italy, a 'legend of elegant courage'.

TOP: *The Picture Gallery in which Bonnie Prince Charlie held a grand ball before his victory at Prestonpans in 1745.*

ABOVE: *The* de jure *King of Scotland, England and Ireland, aged 55, an unfulfilled old man. According to Jacobite sentiment he had been Charles III since his father's death in 1776.*

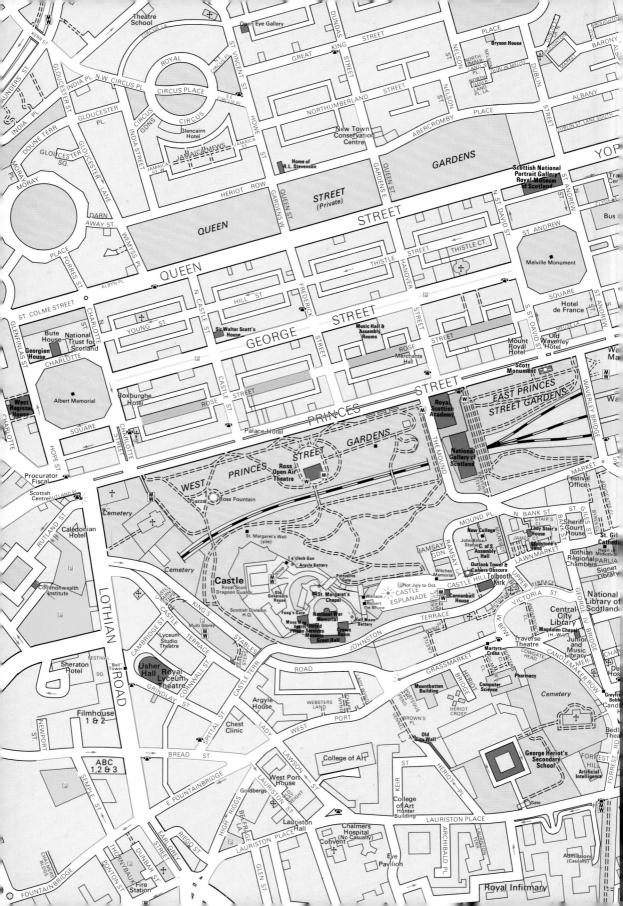

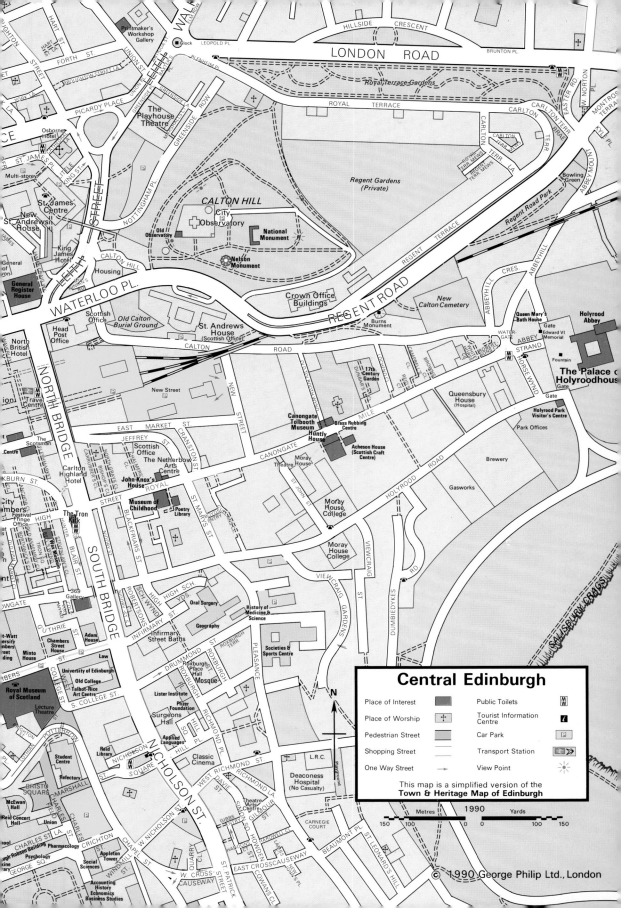

*Tho' many cities have more people in them, yet,
I believe, this may be said with truth, that in no city
in the world so many people live in so little room as
at Edinburgh.*

DANIEL DEFOE, 1724–7

Geography and politics had thrown the people of the old town into close proximity, and if this was not beneficial to the health of Auld Reekie (the city's nickname) it had its effect in the circulation of ideas. These spread up and down the High Street and throughout all classes so that philosophy and poetry belonged as much to the man in the street as to the professor at the University.

Many important and influential men in the world of letters lived on the Royal Mile. Allan Ramsay set up his wig-making business in the High Street, but he was also Ramsay the poet, the collector of songs, and the playwright. In addition, he was a publisher, for which purpose he removed to a site between Borthwick's Close and Old Assembly Close. In Carrubber's Close

ABOVE and RIGHT:
*The High Street,
looking down
towards Canongate.*

on the other side of the High Street, Ramsay built a theatre, which was refused a licence. He ended his days in Ramsay Lodge, a house which he built near to the Castle.

Honest Allan, as he was called, left behind not only his poems and songs, his play *The Gentle Shepherd*, which has been revived at the Edinburgh Festival, but also a son, Allan, whose portrait painting has been increasingly valued over recent years. There are some fine examples in the National Gallery of Scotland.

ABOVE: *The Old Town from Calton Hill.*

LEFT: *Gladstone's Land, a condemned property in the High Street in 1934, was donated to the National Trust for Scotland and restored as a 17th-century Old Town house.*

BELOW, LEFT: *The Green Room, furnished to act as a bridge between the styles of Edinburgh's Old and New Towns.*

BELOW, RIGHT: *The Cloth Merchant's Booth, a reconstruction of the 17th-century shop on the street floor.*

Robert Fergusson, poetic successor to Allan Ramsay senior, died young, and was buried in the churchyard of the Canongate Kirk. There he rests with other famous persons such as Adam Smith – author of *The Wealth of Nations*. Robert Burns commissioned a headstone to be erected to Fergusson.

Up the hill in the Lawnmarket in Craig's Close lived Burns's publisher, William Creech. He was followed by Sir Walter Scott's publisher, Constable. Here came the founders of that severe critical organ, *The Edinburgh Review*, amongst whom was the English wit, the Reverend Sydney Smith. Of the *Review* Mme. de Stael wrote: 'If some being from another climate were to desire to know in what work the highest pitch of intellect might be found, he ought to be shown *The Edinburgh Review*.'

A few yards away is Anchor Close, where William Smellie, a printer, naturalist and antiquary, printed the first edition of *The Encyclopaedia Britannica* in three volumes. Creech brought Burns's poems here to have them printed on the premises and Smellie introduced Burns to The Crochallan Club, one of the many clubs which met for debate, song and entertainment.

Again, within a matter of yards James's Court testifies to the concentration of men of genius. It was there that James Boswell on 14 August 1773 received the message that Dr Samuel Johnson had arrived at Boyd's Inn at the head of the Canongate. It was late but Boswell escorted him up the High Street to his own home, Johnson complaining the while about the stench of the street and remarking 'I smell you in the dark.' The peril of being drenched by foul water thrown from an upper window, so Boswell recorded, was much abated by the enforcement of the laws, though no doubt the old cry 'Gardyloo!' *(gardez l'eau)* could still be heard.

Before Boswell's tenancy of the third floor, it had been occupied by David Hume, the historian and Scotland's most notable philosopher. Of this Age of Enlightenment the American president, Thomas Jefferson, wrote, 'no place in the World can pretend to a competition with Edinburgh.'

ABOVE: *Lady Stair's House, built in 1622, is now a museum exhibiting relics of Robert Burns, Sir Walter Scott and Robert Louis Stevenson.*

LEFT: *The granite blocks of the Heart of Midlothian mark the entrance to the old Tolbooth prison, demolished in 1817.*

ABOVE: *Canongate Kirk, built in 1688 for worshippers displaced when Holyrood Abbey was converted for the use of the Knights of the Thistle. Bonnie Prince Charlie's prisoners from the Battle of Prestonpans in 1745 were confined 'in the Jail and Church of the Canongate'.*

LEFT: *White Horse Close, site of the Royal Mews in the 16th century before White Horse Inns and coaching stables were built in 1623.*

LEFT: *Moray Place, in the New Town.*

BELOW: *A decorative fanlight in Queen Street.*

The impression Edinburgh has made upon us is very great; it is quite beautiful, totally unlike anything else I have seen; and what is even more, Albert, who has seen so much, says it is unlike anything he ever saw.

QUEEN VICTORIA, 1842

George Drummond, six times Lord Provost of Edinburgh, prophesied that one day 'a splendid and magnificent city' would be built to the north of the Old Town. In 1767 the plan for a new town put forward by a young architect, James Craig, was accepted by the Town Council. Rectangular in concept and initially composed of three parallel streets running from east to west – Princes Street, George Street and Queen Street – it was intersected by streets going north and south and framed at the east and west by great squares and crescents; and between the streets were gardens, in which nature and art were brought together. So classical Edinburgh, with its pillars and porticos, decoration and style referring back to ancient Greece and Rome, came to be built – the product of the Age of Reason.

ABOVE: *The Georgian House, a sympathetic restoration by the National Trust for Scotland of No. 7 Charlotte Square.*

RIGHT: *The Parlour in the Georgian House, as it might well have looked in the 18th century.*

LEFT: *An aerial view showing the relationship of the New Town to the Old Town.*

RIGHT, ABOVE: *An ornate ceiling at No. 5, Charlotte Square.*

There are splendid individual buildings throughout the city: the Register House by Robert Adam; the University Buildings on the South Bridge route with their great monolithic pillars of local stone, mainly by Adam; the National Gallery and the Royal Scottish Academy by Playfair; the bold and massive St. Stephen's Church by Playfair; the exquisite St. Andrew's Church with its fine spire by David Kay; and the Royal College of Surgeons, by Playfair, which presents a Roman 'solidity and confidence'. There is pleasure to be found in all these; but when one's eye runs along the great rhythm of Moray Place from pillar to pillar or sees it through the spread of trees in the garden at its centre; or when one walks along the dignified Heriot Row, the severity of its line again softened by trees on its south side; or simply looks at that masterpiece, Charlotte Square, designed by Robert Adam, preferably in the afternoon sun and on the north side and yet again in the presence of trees; one appreciates not only a style of architecture but a style of life.

Above the doorway of number 9 Charlotte Square is the name Joseph Lister. The originator of antiseptic surgery took his bride, the daughter of James Syme, President of the Royal College of Surgeons, to live there. Lister had come to Edinburgh to study under Syme. The marriage drew him further into the community of medical scientists in Edinburgh whose international reputation had been the outcome of co-operation as much as of individual genius. In Playfair's building, the Royal College of Surgeons, can be seen the portraits of three professors, the three

RIGHT, BELOW:
*Robert Adam's
masterpiece of urban
architecture, the
north side of
Charlotte Square,
commissioned in 1791* *to provide a
harmonious
continuation to the
development in the
First New Town.*

Monros, grandfather, father and son, who in turn succeeded to the Chair of Medicine. But amongst all the luminaries humanity must be most grateful to Sir James Young Simpson who introduced the use of chloroform in operations. He has recorded how coming home late one night 'I poured some of the fluid into tumblers, before my assistants, Dr. George Keith and Dr. Duncan and myself . . . we all inhaled the fluid, and were all under the mahogany table in a trice.' So the great discovery was made.

Edinburgh New Town has now endured 200 years of exposure to the weather and is in need of repair. The New Town Conservation Committee seek to conserve the buildings, and their interesting Centre is open to the public at 13A Dundas Street. Guided walks led by experts take place regularly in June, July and August.

BELOW: *The Camera Obscura (Castle Hill) was installed in the Outlook Tower in the 1850s by an optician. In 1945 a superior lens and mirror system was installed and has been in use ever since.*

RIGHT: *The National Gallery of Scotland (The Mound) houses a fine collection of works by Continental and British masters.*

RIGHT, BELOW: *The Royal Botanic Garden (Inverleith Row) was established as a Physic Garden in 1670 and is now the second largest botanic garden in Britain.*

Canongate Tolbooth
Canongate
Built in 1591, a courthouse and prison for 300 years, it is now a museum, displaying Highland dress and tartan.

Edinburgh Castle (see pp.2–5).

The Fruit Market Gallery
Market Street
Both Scottish and international artists are exhibited here.

Huntly House
Canongate
This restored 16th-century town house shows in the decoration of some of its rooms the different styles of life that have taken place within it.

The Georgian House (see p.21).

Gladstone's Land (see p.17).

John Knox's House (see p.7).

Lady Stair's House (see p.18).

National Gallery of Modern Art
Belford Road
Most of the major modern artists and sculptors are represented here along with modern Scottish artists.

CENTRE, RIGHT: *A penguin race at the Edinburgh Zoo (Corstorphine Road). Education and research are paramount in the Zoo's beautiful 80 acres which contain some of the world's rarest animals.*

BELOW, RIGHT: *The Museum of Childhood (High Street) is a treasure-house of toys and objects associated with childhood. Quite possibly 'the noisiest museum in the world', it is certainly fun.*

National Library of Scotland
George IV Bridge
This library has an unrivalled collection of Scottish books and manuscripts.

National Museum of Antiquities of Scotland
Queen Street
Collections showing the history of Scotland from early times to the present day.

National Portrait Gallery
Queen Street
Portraits of important Scottish characters.

Netherbow Arts Centre
High Street
Exhibits works of lesser-known living Scottish artists.

New Town Conservative Centre
Dundas Street
Holds a permanent display of the conservation work in progress on the Georgian New Town.

Palace of Holyroodhouse (see pp.10–13).

The Scottish Experience
Shandwick Place
Two multi-media presentations: a relief map of Scotland and 'The Edinburgh Show' outlining the city's history.

Scottish United Services Museum (see p.5).

This list of Edinburgh's museums, galleries and places of interest is not exhaustive, but gives a taste of the city's cultural richness.

ABOVE: *The Duke of Wellington statue, with the Scott memorial in the background, in Princes Street.*

FAR LEFT, ABOVE: *The galleried interior of Jenner's, Edinburgh's large department store in Princes Street.*

LEFT, ABOVE: *The restored atrium in the Royal Scottish Museum (Chambers Street), housed in one of the finest Victorian buildings in the country; it is an ideal setting for the varied collections.*

LEFT: *Princes Street Gardens, looking up towards the High Street.*

ABOVE: *Edinburgh University, established in 1583, is the sixth oldest in Britain and has over 11,000 full-time students. Its reputation in the fields of medicine and science is pre-eminent and many literary figures have studied there. HRH the Duke of Edinburgh is the present Chancellor.*

BELOW: *Waverley Market, at the Bus Station end of Princes Street, provides varied undercover shopping on several levels.*